Diary of a Mad

FIRST LADY

Diary of a Mad
FIRST LADY

Elisha Boyd

USA

The Author's Pen, LLC
PO Box 720798
Houston, TX 77272
www.tapwriting.com

Scriptures marked NLT are taken from the HOLY BIBLE, NEW LIVING TRANSLATION (NLT): Scriptures taken from the HOLY BIBLE, NEW LIVING TRANSLATION, Copyright© 1996, 2004, 2007 by Tyndale House Foundation. Used by permission of Tyndale House Publishers, Inc., Carol Stream, Illinois 60188. All rights reserved. Used by permission.

Scriptures marked NIV are taken from the NEW INTERNATIONAL VERSION (NIV): Scripture taken from THE HOLY BIBLE, NEW INTERNATIONAL VERSION ®. Copyright© 1973, 1978, 1984, 2011 by Biblica, Inc.™. Used by permission of Zondervan.

Scriptures marked KJV are taken from the KING JAMES VERSION (KJV): KING JAMES VERSION, public domain.

Diary of a Mad First Lady, Elisha Boyd. -- 1st print ed.
ISBN 978-1-948248-06-8

I Wonder

As I sit and wonder, praise and worship fill the air and the claps of your people sounding like thunder as I ponder, why Lord do I bother, why do I care, why am I so concerned as Hallelujah's fill the air. As I sit and I wonder, Lord, should I continue to move forward when it's obvious that many of these claps and praises are not meant for your glory. I sit and wonder, as I scan around the room, the congregation is being so consumed with the praise and the claps of the Raging Thunder of praise and worship, to the beating of the drums I wonder and I wonder is this love really for real? Is this love really what I truly feel? Is this love that I send your way? Is this love really here to stay? As I sit and I wonder!

DEDICATION

I dedicate this book to my Shero, my mother Anita Gail Jacobs and my Hero my father Jimmy L. Jacobs! Thank you for all the love and encouragement through the years. Most of all, thank you for all the sacrifices known and unknown. I love you both and could not have made it without you two in my life.

ACKNOWLEDGMENTS

To the man of God, Pastor Daniel E. Boyd, my loving, wonderful gift from God. You are amazing and my biggest support. I say it often and I will say it to the world, he is my sauce because he keeps me covered. None of this would be possible without your constant support and encouragement. I love you with every fiber of my being!

To my children Nathaniel and Danika, I love you both and have always tried to be the best mother I can be for you both. Thank you for your support, understanding and encouragement during this endeavor.

To my brother J.J., thank you for always being there and believing in me. I love you!

To my Father and Mother in Love, Pastor Jackie and Joyce Boyd, thank you for the love and support as I traveled this journey with your son. You both are such a great inspiration to me. I love you both!

To my grands, Kassidy Boyd and Athena Boyd, you both light up my life with loving thoughts of you even across the miles and no matter what Kassidy you will always be Nana's Peaches, and Athena you will always be Nana's little Toot Toot!

To my spiritual parents, Bishop M.L. Jackson and Lady S.L. Jackson, thank you for believing in the God in me, all the love and support you both have shown towards me, my family and ministry.

To my mentor, Dr. Mary Murray, thank you for taking me under your wing and helping me birth this book through your dynamic Coaching School.

To my ECC family and W.O.W. Women, you guys are absolutely the best!!! We live, love, cry, praise and worship together. I salute you and thank you for all you do for me and my family. Let's continue to live our life principle being a church that loves God and loves God's people! I love you all!

To the ladies that contributed to the survey, thank you all so very much.

To my ride and live friend and everyone that backed my funding campaign, thank you for your sacrifice and support. May God Bless you all!

CONTENTS

Lady SL Jackson

In the increasing complexity and ever evolving dynamics of the Christian Church Leadership across denominational lines, it is imperative that some of the major challenges that pastor wives incur as they *minister* alongside the God chosen under shepherd be addressed. Unfortunately, many women find themselves clueless when their husband is called to pastor or to other places of leadership.

In this book, *Diary of a Mad First Lady,* the author shares some of the wisdom that was imparted to help her as she stepped into the role of first lady of a new ministry. Her willingness to reveal not only the success but also the challenges she endured as the Lord transformed her into the *Help* that was needed for her husband. That is key, no two ministries are alike. Each pastor's wife will have to allow God and her husband to define her role. The most important thing that we as pastor wives, must be diligent in cultivating, is our relationship with God first. Then, we must understand that we are wife first, and first lady second. Our role as wife as outlined in Genesis 3:18, is to be a *help* suitable to the man God has placed in our lives. Each man and his ministry are uniquely created by God; therefore, the role of each pastor's wife will be different. As help we must: honor him, encourage him, love him and especially pray for him.

I have had the blessed pleasure of watching the author, Elisha Boyd; grow from a new babe to a dynamic Woman of God, Entrepreneur and now Author. Having seen the hand of God working in her life for almost twenty years, it does not surprise me the things God has and will continue to do with her. I believe that this book will be an inspiration and an encouragement to women around the world.

Lady SL Jackson

My Story

I WAS BORN IN CHARLOTTE, NC and raised in a rural town better known as Turkeytown. And, no! Before you start wondering, there are absolutely no turkeys in Turkeytown. I attended Gaston High School where I was a stellar athlete and an exceptional student. Upon receiving a basketball scholarship, I worked so hard to get, I set out to college ready to begin my journey as a Lady Mustang at the University of Alabama in Huntsville. This is where my life took a great turn. I was in a city with freedom and tons of temptation; young and dumb is what I say now.

Many things happened during my Mustang journey. I was tempted and became prey for many of my tempters such as fornication, lesbianism, alcoholism, drugs and more. When you go down those dark allies, it seems almost impossible to

3

turn around, even when you become the victim of unwanted and unwelcomed sexual traumas in your life. These events leave you empty, numb and can cause you to become callous, therefore building an emotional wall so tall and thick it is impossible for anyone or anything to break through. The truth of the matter, I was looking for a way of escape, so I could break free from the hurt, guilt and shame I felt deep down inside.

Many people feel that a person has to pour their insides out to someone to get relief. I found it is okay to trust in a friend or family member however, sometimes the traumatic event is so hurtful and shameful you feel you have nobody to turn to that will understand. After years of carrying the weight on my shoulders of being raped, abused and sexually harassed during the early part of my tenure in the United States Army; I got to know a man that I could go to with all my scars and wounds.

I tried to treat myself, not willing to reach out to the people I *knew* I could trust because of past hurt from those I *thought* I could trust. I turned to alcohol and men to mask my pain, now isn't that a hoot. The very thing that got me in the bed with the devil is the very thing I turned to but this time I was controlling the shots or, so I thought. I developed the motto, *I'm going to get them before they get me.*

One day the weight became so heavy until I couldn't bare it anymore. I started attending church and one Sunday was like no other. I prayed, and I asked the Lord, "If you save me and deliver me from drinking, take the taste from my mouth immediately and deliver me from the club, I will serve you." That was twenty years ago and I'm still serving God. Now, does it mean I got it right all the time, every time? The answer is NO! Things never go according to our plan until we line up with the will of God for our lives and come to the realization that it is not about us or our plans. When we operate of our plan and ours alone, it may work out and then again it may not, especially in the church.

Now, whoever is reading this may be wondering, *why are you mad*? I'm getting to that, keep reading.

In the Beginning

IN THE BEGINNING of my journey I wasn't very receptive to receiving help and I didn't have many friends because I had an issue with having female friends. I wasn't as outgoing as people perceived me to be. I found myself becoming more of a loner because I was trying to find out who I was becoming and how I fit into my husband's life. I would like to do things by myself even when people would see me doing something or putting together an activity, I wouldn't welcome the help. My answer was *no thank you, I got it.* I began to focus on how I could become better once I married a minister because I understood my walk needed to complement his.

I attended a women's ministry session at the church where my husband served as youth pastor. The session was geared around your appearance inside and out. The facilitator discussed what we should and shouldn't wear according to our shape, height and weight. We discussed hairstyles that complimented the shape of your face, makeup shoes, even on how you should sit down. This class helped me because I wore dresses occasionally, but preferred pants and I never thought how my wardrobe spoke volumes as to who I was at that point. I was a soldier and wore a uniform most of the time. The thought of dressing up and focusing on hair and makeup wasn't my thing. My take on it was, *you either except me in this uniform or you don't except me at all!*

Gradually, I began to turn things up a notch, and when I did, I received some shocking feedback from my support team. Some of them who were very close to me told me that I was changing because I started wearing suites instead of dresses or pants and a blouse. Someone said, "Just because you are married to the youth pastor doesn't mean you have to wear a suite."

I was completely blown away by their reaction. I tried to explain that wasn't the case at all, I called myself mirroring the only example I had before me, which was my first lady. There was some distance that began to grow between us however I thank God, he answers prayer. I didn't understand it, couldn't understand it; all I knew was if anybody should understand me it should be them. They came to me and told me they were wrong and apologized and they realized I wasn't changing, I was merely stepping into my role as the youth pastor's wife. My support team and I were back together again ready to take on the youth and the world. They were all I had, which consisted of two individuals within the church helping me stay focused and holding me accountable. As the years passed, we grew in terms of support and others came aboard the team again holding me accountable and reassuring me they were there to support not only me but the youth pastor as well.

The mother's board, now they were absolutely the sweetest. They all had pearls of wisdom to share with me from how to cook for him, supporting him in ministry and at home, and how to keep him at home. One of mothers told me, "Now baby, be a lady in the street and a freak in the bedroom because whatever you did to get him baby you got to keep doing it to keep him." My whole perspective of the mother's board was changed. They may have some gray hair and some age on them, but they weren't slow at all. Unbelievable right?

It gets better. I received some shocking advice from a friend and mentor in the church. She's a woman of God, a pillar in the community, seasoned pastor's wife with years of serving under her belt who has been, and still is a blessing to me and my family. Pastor wives, minister wives and women in general, are you ready for this one? She said, "When you really want to get your husband's attention because there will come a time in the marriage when he is going to be glued to the television and not to you, all you have to do is start vacuuming." My facial expression must have said it all because her response was, "you do know how to vacuum don't you?" I said, "Yes ma'am, but I don't see how that is going to make him stop watching TV." I wasn't ready for her response, "That means you are not vacuuming the right way." She began to give me instructions which were:

"First, you've got to dress appropriately. Don't wear anything, let it all hang out. Next, use the attachment so you can get the dust from the top of the curtains and vacuum way up high. Next, you switch it out and vacuum way down low in front of the TV as low as you can go, and I guarantee you will have his attention. See I told you, you didn't know how to vacuum." I hollered, "Oh Lord!!!" Can you imagine the look on my face when she finished? I promise you these are true stories and many of them blessed me even if I didn't know how to vacuum. I can assure you I never looked at vacuuming the same. The moral of the story is you need that support from those that have been where you are trying to go. As we grew with each other, in the ministry and our faith, the Lord had other plans for my husband and me.

The day came that I never really thought would happen, my husband came home one day and told me the Lord was calling him to pastor. My thought was okay, you are the full-time youth pastor in a rural area where that is almost unheard of in small towns. If you leave that job what are we going to do? I was in school and working but my income was not enough to sustain us.

All my natural senses kicked in. And, can I be transparent? My exact words to him, "I need you to go back down and make sure it's the Lord!" If it is the Lord, then okay I will support you one hundred percent; but it better be the Lord because we got mouths to feed, bills to pay. I went in on him instead of supporting him and praying, initially. The Lord brought correction, so I had to humble myself and pray with him and for him for direction and wisdom. We were part of a thriving ministry, my church home where I received my salvation and deliverance, so I wasn't just trying to roll out like that. My baby's friends were there, my friends were there, that ministry was all I knew for almost ten years. Now, you are asking me to leave my support system, my comfort zone and follow you into the wilderness? In my mind, that's where we were headed. Fear and uncertainty gripped me because we would be embarking on this journey alone; and as the elders use to say in the church I was reared in as a little girl, it was time for us to work out our own salvation with fear and trembling.

Prayer was definitely in order and as I went to the Lord in prayer I found myself not praying for what I felt needed to happen but for the will of God to be done in our lives. I prayed for him to give direction to his son, the man of God and I will follow. God gave me a peace about it and prepared my heart. When the time came for us to take the giant leap of faith, we were met with criticism. It wasn't the most popular decision for some and others didn't believe it, couldn't understand it and many were glad about it. None of these things swayed our determination to please God by walking in obedience to him.

Did it cost us some things? Yes, it did. We learned a lot about who was really for us and who was not. In situations like this, God will show you who really has a vested interest in you and who are only interested in what you have to bring to the table. Starting a ministry from ground zero was something we never experienced or been a part of, so there was no real physical support group in the beginning. Our parents were concerned as well as our friends who were supporting us in prayer. We had no money, no resources, no building; it was just us! We had bible study in our living room; my husband, myself and our daughter. Then, before we knew it we started receiving phone calls from different people; including four of our close friends that had been with us in ministry that knew we were taking a leap of faith and shared that the Lord released them to come and be a part of what God was doing through us.

We sought God in prayer together petitioning him for direction and he spoke one night in prayer that he was sending us out from among our place of contentment and sending us to unfamiliar territory to start the ministry. We embraced what God said and prepared ourselves to transition the ministry, but we would stay in our home and just commute for a while as he led us to Richmond Hill, GA. Once we stepped out in faith and secured a store front facility, God went to work, and the people began to come. He sent those that did not have a problem supporting us in ministry and those that would help hold up my husband's arms as the Senior Pastor in the middle of this process.

We met many obstacles trying to secure a location such as racism and bigotry when some Caucasian pastors realized we were planning to establish our ministry in that area. One pastor made it very plain that he was not willing to be a part of the change in community ministerial organizations therefore resigned from his leadership position. We continued to move the vision forward despite how the welcome wagon that was initially rolled out had stopped running. It was disheartening to see my husband have to go through that, but I remained steadfast in prayer. The ministry came together as Pastor initiated our intercessory prayer ministry and we moved some chains in the spirit. As of the time of writing this book, God has kept us for nine years and blessed us to acquire land to build a community and impact the city with the help of our strong support team.

CHAPTER TWO

Relationship, Communication & *Constructive* Criticism

NOW THAT I HAVE finished shouting and praising God for the man of God finding me and accepting me in the flawed state I was in, let's talk about *Relationship, Communication* and *Criticism*. My husband met me in a fragile state because I was just getting to know God, and with tears in my eyes, I can wholeheartedly say the Lord blessed me with my husband. God allowed us to come together on one accord and work in ministry as husband and wife while serving in the Youth Ministry.

I was the youth director and he became the youth pastor shortly after joining the ministry. We knew each other from a few years earlier. Remember, I told you all I was a soldier and I was accustomed to telling soldier what to do, not them telling me what to do. So here it is, the roles were reversed and I'm taking direction and guidance from someone who was my friend, now youth pastor, who ends up being my husband. I know, Wow! I will say it for you, *who does that?* God does that. I didn't know it then, but I know it now.

During the time while we befriended each other, neither one of us had the thought in our mind things were going to turn out like they did. I look back on it now and realize God was in the plan since the beginning of our meeting. I wasn't the nicest person when our paths first crossed, God was still working and building me. The truth is, God was building our relationship and I never thought about it like that. He may have but I didn't see it.

Relationship

Relationship is the state of being connected by blood or marriage and can also be referred to as a romantic or passionate attachment. Our relationship started as an interpersonal relationship. That is a strong, deep, or close association or acquaintance between two or more people that may range in duration from brief to enduring. What started out as a friendship became a commitment to be life partners and endure the good, bad and the ugly no matter what. That is what we believe, and we continue to believe the same way to this day. In October we will celebrate *twenty years* of marriage if the Lord delay his coming. Has it been years of blissful marriage? No, it has not, but it has been almost twenty years of great conversation, commitment, struggles, making up, support and loving each other through our flaws and imperfections.

On this journey as first ladies, a strong relationship with your husband is your lifeline and vital to your survival as the first lady. It is the single most important advice I can admonish you to adhere to other than having a very strong prayer life. Your relationship with your husband, the pastor, is key in the home, the support of the ministry, family the few people we consider friends, and more importantly, to those that don't know you. Why?

Like I stated earlier, everyone is watching you and your family just waiting to see who is going to mess up and where is the scandal going to come from. People love to entertain drama, that's why we see so much of it today during prime-time television. A strong, working relationship with your husband is a must whether you are walking beside him in ministering the Gospel or you are standing beside him cheering him on. You should be his biggest fan and loudest cheerleader, and nobody, I mean nobody should beat you in lifting him up, encouraging him, especially when he is ministering the word of God.

People respond to him how you respond to him. I tried it myself because the same tidbit was shared with me. The majority of the time if you say amen the people will say amen, if you stand up and clap the people will stand up and clap. Try it one Sunday if you haven't, and watch. Be sure to tell me the results.

You not only need a strong relationship, you need a healthy relationship. A healthy relationship is one that you keep building and building on. When your leaders and lay members see you and your husband together they should see and feel you're genuine. What you do affects others around you and that can be negative or positive. It depends on you two working together which encourages those ladies that may not have that genuine affection in their relationship. It gives them hope that it is possible.

Relationship, Communication, Constructive Criticism

Speaking the same language as much as possible is a great compliment to you both, however it can be a difficult task to master. Mastering the task of communication can be accomplished once a clear understanding of what communication really is and entails has been established within the relationship. Often, I think there is a misconception about how to communicate with one another as we walk out this journey.

Communication

Communication is not one person doing all the talking and the other person just listening. Communication is not shouting and yelling, trying to outtalk each other to get your point across. Communication is not talking at each other or down to one another, diminishing the value of each other thoughts. I can continue to tell you a laundry list of what it is not, but more importantly, I want to share with you what it is and the importance of effective communication when it involves the pastor and the first lady of the church. Ladies, we love to express ourselves verbally and we know most men are the opposite. Just because God called them to pastor a church he didn't say they were going to stop their manly ways and attributes.

--

The first point I would like to make is, he is your husband not your son. Even if you think at times that he is acting like his offspring, I assure you, he is a man. You should not treat your husband in that manner. If you do, it is not going to be productive for you or the ministry because your husband will not welcome it or receive it. This is where effective communication has its place in the relationship. You want your relationship to not only survive, you want it to thrive. Make communication a building block you work on daily in your relationships with your spouse and the people God placed in your care and life.

Effective communication is verbal speech or other methods of relaying information that get a point across. For example, effective communication *is when the person who you are talking to listens actively, absorbs your point and understands it.* We know this stuff, it's not new but the more comfortable we get within our relationships, the more our style of communication decreases.

Listening is a huge part of communicating with your spouse. If you, as his wife doesn't listen and take directions from your husband, why would you think the people of God are going to do something you are not doing. If you are contradicting everything he says and does, then the people are going to think they can do the same thing. You help validate your husband just as much as he validates you and your role in ministry.

I've heard it said, "I don't do it in front of the people, I wait until I get home to tell him what I think. It's wrong first ladies because that is not how you handle the man of God." I used to think the same thing. As long as I didn't embarrass him in front of people or if he did something I didn't like, I would say wait until we get home. Get home and you go in only for it to blow up in your face. And who has to apologize for their actions? You do! If anything like that happens, you can take a different approach to the situation.

Examine the situation and ask God how to approach him about your feelings while keeping your husband's feelings in mind. You don't want him to get upset or take it the wrong way. The word of God teaches us in Colossians 4:6, "Let your conversation be gracious and attractive so that you will have the right response for everyone." I have found that when you stop, think, pray then act; things work out a whole lot better than just setting things off at that moment your feelings are hurt. You try your best to hold true to approaching things with an open mind and heart, however it is not a perfect world and it doesn't always end as such. Rome was not built in a day. It takes work and commitment so when intense moments of fellowship arise, you will have a blueprint to get back on track.

Did you know your ability to listen makes up 40% of the communication process? Talking makes up 35%, reading 16% and writing 9%. This breakdown illustrates the time we spend on each aspect of the communication process. If you can master being an effective listener, it increases your interpersonal communication, professional growth and career satisfaction. I haven't always been a good listener when it came to my husband because I was accustomed to being the person in charge and telling people what to do, so it was difficult for me to listen to him in the beginning of our journey together. Thanks be to God, I'm a hundred times better with communicating effectively which helps me to accept constructive criticism from my husband.

--

Constructive Criticism

Accepting constructive criticism from our husbands can be another area of difficulty because we have gotten comfortable in our relationship.

Constructive criticism *is a recommended set of instructions that aims to collaboratively improve the overall quality of a product or service. Often containing helpful and specific suggestions for positive change, constructive criticism is highly focused on a particular issue or set of issues, as opposed to providing general feedback on the item or organization as a whole.*

Godly criticism is to give a corrective evaluation of another person and their service to the Lord with the intent of helping that person grow in faithfulness to God.

When we are operating in our role alongside our husband in ministry, we strive to do our best to the point of perfection because we serve an excellent God. We want our light to shine and God to be glorified in the process. We may, at times, get a little side tracked and irritated by the way things are unfolding. Our husbands are observing us just as we are observing them and giving them advice as to what we think or how we think things should flow in the ministry. They listen, but may not agree all the time, which can cause us to be a little uneasy, especially when he says, "I don't see what you are saying, or I don't agree with you doing it like that."

When he offers suggestions as to how you can do the same thing but go a different route, do you get mad and keep doing it your way, or do you listen to the man of God? Okay, I will answer first. I didn't always listen in the beginning and wanted things to go my way because I felt if God shared it with me, then we should do it my way. My attitude was so stank about some things, to the point that I was going to do it my way or not at all. I'm helping somebody right here. I knew of constructive criticism but did not know how to handle it.

Just because God may have given you the idea it doesn't mean it has to be carried out by you and you alone. Enlisting the help of others goes a long way, especially when it is your life partner. It hurts us more when our husbands don't agree with us just because of who he is to us. We must also realize our husbands are not sabotaging what we are trying to do. He wants to help and enhance our ideas. He has an obligation to you as your husband however, he also has an obligation to the ministry as well. This dual role can be difficult on many occasions, but this is when you as the first lady must breathe and say, "He is my pastor as well as my husband, so I will accept and respect what he is saying to me."

Constructive criticism is important, it makes us better and stronger. When God gives you instructions on how to carry out His plan and who to assist you, it is needed for the success of the vision, in ministry, in the home as well and our individual lives. I'm at a point now in my life that I welcome constructive criticism because I don't know it all and two brains are better than one. I know my husband's input is positive and helpful to me, and whatever I'm trying to do he will not allow me to embarrass myself or others.

This is important in ministry because people want authenticity and realness, plus they want to be involved and have a voice as well. Address the Ladies in your women's ministry, be as transparent as you can be, and welcome constructive criticism from them. You never know who is siting among you and how God will use them to turn an ordinary idea into something extraordinary because you allowed room for constructive criticism.

Your ability as the first lady to handle constructive criticism from your husband while working by his side in ministry sends a very strong message to the people of God that serve with you. In everything that we do we want to do it God's way using Godly wisdom. Proverbs 27:17 NLT says, "As iron sharpens iron, so a friend sharpens a friend." If it is our desire for people to grow, we must offer criticism with love. If we desire to see people to grow, we must offer criticism with love instead of keeping silent because we don't want to offend anyone or hurt their feelings, and vice versa.

What greater example can you be than walking together in wholeness with your husband? You have to be the living example for the people of God. Being under the microscope of someone else is tough, and the truth is, people criticize everything people do and say whether you are a pastor, first lady or lay member; it doesn't matter. They are going to offer their opinion whether you hear them say it or not. It is the people that respect you enough and the position God has placed you in that will love you enough to offer Godly wisdom to you and not talk about you when service ends.

Relationship, Communication, Constructive Criticism

This is a key element in keeping your marital relationship healthy as well as the health of the church. If we can't offer Godly wisdom in love, then we are not helping each other grow and be the best we can be to God and for His Kingdom. Then, you must ask yourself, why am I doing what I do if I can't receive help which means I'm not in a position to help anyone else?

Everything I do I take very seriously, as I imagine you do as well. Know that as I know better, I purpose in my heart to do better. First ladies, you want the ministry to grow and not be stagnant and stinking, you want to experience spiritual growth for yourself and the people of God you serve, so stop being offended so easily and know that your husband is infallible in your eye sight.

My husband is my best friend and I will always cherish the growth in our relationship as we continue to build our life together while helping build people along the way. If it were not for Pastor Daniel Boyd and his constructive criticism, I definitely would not be who I am in God today.

CHAPTER THREE

Supporting Your Husband

A STRONG DESIRE TO SUPPORT your husband in what God has called him to do is imperative. Your desire to support him in ministry will be so strong until it becomes a yearning because you want to see him succeed. Ladies, you know when you really want that piece of chocolate cake and it keeps calling your name? And, no matter how many times you say *no, I'm not going to eat it* and you eat it anyway; that is the type of desire I'm trying to express to you. This desire will cause you to want to meet every need that may arise because the members may be few and you want to help your husband as much as possible, keeping him free from added stress. Your desire should always be one that will help and complement your husband in ministry while not losing who you are or trying to please people. Your desire is to help and support your husband, and to do it by pleasing God according to Galatians 1:10 NLT. It reads, "Obviously, I'm not trying to win the approval of people, but of God. If pleasing people were my goal, I would not be Christ's servant."

Your husband confirms your dreams and visions by welcoming your desire and commitment to serve right by his side in ministry. He is the Pastor and God can and will use him to validate who you are and what you are called to do in the ministry you are planted in. Don't be surprised if he begins to probe and throw questions at you just to see where your heart is and where you may serve the ministry best. My husband told me before we were married, the Lord showed him in a vision a woman standing beside him and spoke the word *Evangelist*. That truly was a turning point for me and served as a green light to move forward in ministry with my husband. Being called by God is a High Privilege and being validated and supported by your husband makes it that much sweeter as you use your works to enhance the Pastor.

Diary of a Mad First Lady

Every first lady is not called to minister the gospel alongside her husband, however I believe if you are a pastor's wife there is a level of support that needs to be shown toward the man of God and the ministry.

CHAPTER FOUR

Understanding the Role of First Lady

THERE ARE THREE INGREDIENTS I would like to share to help you understand your role: your prayers are vital to the success of your husband's ministry; your home is your first ministry and love the people of God. In my opinion, this is the recipe for success.

When I married into ministry, I must admit fear gripped me. I didn't know what to expect. My husband was a youth pastor, and although I had been working in ministry prior to our meeting, I still didn't know how my role would change as the youth pastor's wife. My first lady began to share with me the importance of praying for my husband consistently. She said, "The best advice I can give you is, make the altar your friend." Honestly, I didn't quite get it the first few years but as time progressed and we embarked on our journey as pastors of what is now Emmanuel Christian Church those words became more relevant.

Your Prayers are Vital to the Success of Your Husband's Ministry

It is my belief that prayer is the key and faith unlocks the door. Don't be afraid to go to the altar, make the altar your friend.

There will be times when all you are going to be able to do is pray and hold on to your faith as you trust God to move on your behalf. On this journey, your prayer life must be a lifestyle. Lifting your husband before God, asking Him to lead, guide and protect the man of God and your children becomes normal. Believing God to provide all that is needed, so the ministry will not go lacking in any area but will be the beacon light in the community.

John 14: 12-14 NLT says, "I tell you the truth, anyone who believes in me will do the same works I have done, and even greater works, because I am going to be with the Father. You can ask for anything in my name, and I will do it, so that the Son can bring glory to the Father. Yes, ask me for anything in my name, and I will do it!"

Your Home is Your First Ministry

No matter what goes on in the ministry, your first ministry is your home; especially if you have small children. Some time ago, a good family friend passed away and we attended her funeral in Griffin, GA. While sitting at a table during the repass, a beautiful woman sat across from me and started a conversation. It began with small talk and then she asked me if she could share something with me. She said, "I use to be the first lady of this church, but my husband passed away last year and now I'm just a member. I raised all five of my children right here in this church, but they are grown now." Then, she went on to say jokingly, "I was probably the worst first lady they ever had." My eyes were as wide as fifty cent pieces; I had no idea what was coming next. She asked me what I did in the church and I replied by running off my list of roles: youth director, youth leader, wife and mother.

She looked at our daughter and said, "Is that your baby?" I replied, "Yes ma'am."

She said, "You see that beautiful baby girl right there? That is your first ministry. Taking care of your home is first, then church because you will never get these years back. Be a wife and a mother first, and God will honor that. Your husband can't be effective in ministry if he's concerned about his wife and children. They need stability and a home cooked meal; both of you can't be out of the home all the time. Once my children got grown and gone, then I assumed the role of first lady and did what I needed to do."

This is some of the best advice I received second to prayer. It helped me put everything in perspective, and to re-alize that it is okay to miss a service and be there making memories with my children. People may say you are the *worst* first lady, but your children will cast their vote for you as best mom.

Love the People of God

Love covers a multitude of sin. God loved us so very much that he sacrificed his only son to die for us on the cross, so we can be clothed in righteousness. Yes, people can be rude, they can be manipulating, they talk bad about our husbands when they do not agree with them, they talk about our children being spoiled and tell the members not to say anything to our children because *you know how the first lady is about her children*. No, they may not tithe and give of their time and talents like they should according to the word of God. No, they may be inconsistent in attendance and expect the pastor, our husbands to show up when they call. Does this hurt you to see your husband go through these things? Yes! Not only does it hurt, but it makes you and me angry.

The scripture says you can be angry but do not sin and don't allow these negative emotions to consume you or cause bitterness to take up residence. God did not place you in the role of first lady to be concerned about what people do or don't do. He placed you beside your husband to be the *help meet*. You can do so much more for your husband and the ministry if you allow the love that God placed in you for the people to flow. Stop allowing yourself to be grieved by people's actions.

"Most important of all, continue to show deep love for each other, for love covers a multitude of sins." 1 Peter 4:8 NLT

Why are these Things Significant?

I value what God has called me to do and I believe if you are going to do anything, do it wholeheartedly and be the best you can be. I'm a veteran of the United States Army where I served on active duty for thirteen years. I served in man's army, therefore the same principles I learned back in 1989 are the same principles I stand on today, "Be all you can be. I'm just doing it God's way now."

Simply put, when you give God your best he will do the rest. Matthew 6:33 NLT says, "Seek the Kingdom of God above all else, and live righteously, and he will give you everything you need." When you put God first, it makes it easy to keep your husband in prayer, manage the home, care for the children and ultimately love God's people.

Understanding the role of first lady is just like preparing a Thanksgiving meal for your loved ones. You put a lot of time and thought in menu planning, so you can shop for the right ingredients and get everything you need to make each dish. You prepare a delicious meal, set the table and arrange for everyone to enjoy time with family and great food. It is no different than preparing your heart for prayer, faith and love to do ministry effectively and produce a product that God can be pleased with.

Encouragement in Your Role

Forget about your past, it is just that, your past. Why keep looking back when you have so much in front of you to look forward to and to live for. I've discovered when you dwell on the things that are old and irrelevant, your present, relevant state of existence becomes tainted with your past thoughts and actions. Stop allowing the enemy to assist you in selling yourself short by bringing up past issues that cause you to feel inadequate.

Let me encourage you right here. God knows you were a mess, a failure at some things, had some mishaps and misfortunes. he knows. He knows some of you fornicated, had an abortion, committed adultery, smoked weed and any other shortcoming the enemy will throw at you, but leave it in the past. Even when he whispers, you aren't smart enough, you're too big, you aren't pretty enough, your hair isn't long enough, you can't remember scriptures, you don't have what it takes, and any other shameful and painful memories he may try to use against you. Don't believe the lie of the enemy. I say to you first lady, "NO MORE EXCUSES!"

What I didn't realize in the beginning was God already knew me even before I was conceived in my mother's womb. I have heard and read that scripture numerous times but one day I had a spiritual awakening.

The Lord reminded me of the day my husband asked me to marry him and my response to him was I *need to pray about it.* I called my first lady and said, "Lady Jackson! This boy done asked me to marry him. Why me? I'm all excited, hyped up and a nervous wreck; and all I can think about is he is the youth pastor. I am not ready for that! So, why me, why God?" She calmly said to me, "Lady, why not you?" Immediately, I ranted on and on with every excuse I could imagine as to why I wasn't the *one,* but she remained persistent with her question, "Why not you?"

I called my mother only for her to say the same thing. I took that as a sign from the Lord and went in prayer about my answer. After much prayer, the revelation came to me, and I said to myself *why not me? What's so bad about me that I can't marry the man of God?* I began to reassure myself that I was enough. I had the qualities that would complement him and his ministry. According to Proverbs 18:22 NLT, "The man who finds a wife finds a treasure, and he receives favor from the LORD." He knew just who I needed and when I needed him. It was in God's plan because he knew he would place me in a position of influence and authority that allows me to be a blessing to my husband and others in his Kingdom. Bishop T.D. Jakes said it best in his book *God's Leading Lady*, "It's time to shed ex-cues and excuses and magnify what the Lord has planted in you: the seed to be His Leading Lady." If you can do that then there is no doubt that being a first lady will be both fulfilling and rewarding.

Accept the present, you are here now in the glass bowl therefore it is no turning back. Although this may not be something you asked for in life (at least I didn't), God has a way of hurdling us to the place he desires for us to be whether we want to or not. We find ourselves leading and guiding others in our leadership roles and in ministry which challenges our very soul, at times. Nevertheless, we have a job to do and we cannot be effective in our roles unless we are willing to accept what God is allowing to happen. And believe it or not, it is for our good and the greater good of all mankind.

Remember when you were growing up and had dreams, goals and aspirations to do great things. Well ladies, guess what? That little girl is still there on the inside just waiting for those very dreams to come alive. Don't let your dreams go unfulfilled because life happened. Use the platform God has provided and go forth and do great things. My great thing may not be your great thing however there is greatness in you and the time is now to accept the present. Often, we wait to move forward with what the Lord has given us to do because of doubt, fear and procrastination; or believe we must experience a significant emotional event to provoke us to take the giant leap of faith and pursue our dreams. Every day you wait is a moment of your life that you won't get back, so maximize the moment and live up to your potential by maximizing the life God has blessed you with.

To accept the present, you must also eliminate some things and relationships from your life, such as excuses, negative relationships and debt. We are in the final rehearsal of life before Jesus returns, don't you want to make the most of it by rekindling the passion you once had for singing, dancing, modeling, acting? Okay, so maybe not all of those, I had to laugh myself. There was a time when I wanted to be an actress and TV star in the sitcom *Living Single*. I wanted to play the role of Max because she was no nonsense and had the freedom to live life while making a difference in the courtroom. The same attributes I liked then, I like now. Although my acting career never hit the big screen of Hollywood, God allowed me to use those attributes in ministry by exercising the liberty, authority and power he gave us when he shed his blood on the cross and redeemed us back to our father in heaven. I can sing, dance, model and act in God's Kingdom theatre. Grab hold of where God has positioned you, invest in your right now, embrace who you are and the moments to come as you ponder your desires for your future as first lady. It is your time to shine. "Arise shine: for your light has come! And the glory of the Lord is risen upon you!" Isaiah 60:1 NIV

Embrace your future, your future is before you and waiting on you to reach up and grab it. Your soul yearns for a greater tomorrow and you compose a symphony of solutions to your road map designed in your mind to get you to that happy place called the future. The more you engage the dreams and ideas God has given you, the sooner you will see manifestation. As first lady you can have big dreams. As the psalmist said, "Forget about yesterday, learn from your mistakes and move forward."

I, like many of you, have had people talk about me to others within and out of the ministry, lie on me to my friends and family, try to discredit my name, friends turn their backs on me and friends not willing to forgive when I make a mistake. Not to mention, people have come and faded away from the ministry without so much as a good bye, but I have made up in my mind that I'm going to work through it all. I will work through the disappointment, guilt, heartache and pain by working the word of God, so it will work for me. The word of God teaches how to forgive and how to love, and that is what I choose. Living and dwelling on the past delays your growth and holds you hostage from your future. God has placed us center stage in his Kingdom theatre, now it's time to act like you want it and go get it. Be the model you dreamed of because the ladies in your circle and territory are watching you. Be the best model you can be in your role as first lady from your relationship with your husband, children, family, friends, congregants and coworkers. Set the example and lead the way in being fit spiritually, and holistically. Allow God to carry you as far as he wants to take you as you embrace every spiritual awakening moment as you release all the things you thought you buried deep down inside that hindered you and caused your fire not to smolder. Take the

limits off God and tap into your creative ability by going be-
yond the familiar, embracing the unfamiliar and doing
extraordinary things. Somebody is reading this right now and
desires to write a book, a play, be a great artist, recording
artist or desires to be a better first lady. What are you waiting for? Start writing, start drawing, start recording and start
walking in the shoes as you fulfill your role as first lady.

"I don't mean to say that I have already achieved
these things or that I have already reached perfection. But I
press on to possess that perfection for which Christ Jesus first
possessed me. No, dear brothers and sisters, I have not
achieved it, [a] but I focus on this one thing: Forgetting the
past and looking forward to what lies ahead, I press on to
reach the end of the race and receive the heavenly prize for
which God through Christ Jesus, is calling us." Philippians
3:12-14 NLT

Called to Serve

SERVING IN MINISTRY is something that I honestly feel everyone should do because we all are called by God to be servants. Being a servant leader is a place in ministry that many first ladies may find themselves. This is often true when you are building a ministry from ground zero and your membership has yet to flourish.

My story may be a tad different than others. About a year prior to me becoming reacquainted with Daniel Boyd back then he was a soldier I knew, I was having these dreams of me standing before a crowd of people speaking to them and they began to get more vivid each time. The scene in the dream began to change, and the first time I saw myself preaching from the pulpit I woke quickly from my sleep and dismissed it thinking it was something I ate. I couldn't go back to sleep because I was terrified. Preaching was not on my accomplishment list, I was a sinner and I knew there was no sugar coating it. I was in the church working in a ministry, but the church was not in me. So, the last thing I could ever see myself doing was preaching the word of God. Reminds me of a passage in the book Daniel where it reads, "But one night I had a dream that frightened me; I saw visions that terrified me as I lay in my bed." Daniel 4:5 NLT

When it was time to go to sleep, I would ask God *please don't let me see that dream, I want to dream about something happy;* but it didn't happen. I gave in to the Lord and said, "Okay, God okay! Is that what you will have me to do?" Then, I gave him a whole laundry list of why I really wasn't a good candidate to preach his word. "Lord I can't do it, you know I still have a few glasses of wine, I don't know scripture, I can't remember scripture, I don't like wearing dresses like that and who wants to choke themselves with that collar I see priests wear? Matter of fact, God you know I don't even like people like that, my tongue is too sharp, so I'm good without preaching. Keep working on me, Lord and who knows maybe one day I will be ready." After my sarcastic rounds of excuses, I thought the dreams would stop, but they didn't. It wasn't until I met my husband that I didn't have those dreams for a long time.

Why did I wrestle with this? Working in ministry is a serious commitment, if you are going to serve in the capacity God calls you, you must do it wholeheartedly. I didn't feel like I had what it took to make a long-term commitment. Daniel and I started dating and the dreams stopped, which I thought was weird, but hey I was perfectly fine with that. It wasn't until he asked me to marry him that I understood why I had those dreams. He was a minister and was in the position of the youth pastor at that time, and we worked in the Youth Ministry together where I served as youth director. I will never forget this moment as long as I live. I was sitting in church and I looked up and it was as if the Lord opened up a portal, and in that portal, he showed me sitting beside my husband studying the word together. I'm pleased to say that was my answer. Shortly after, we married and celebrate twenty years of marriage. He's still my husband, *my sauce* because he keeps me covered. The Lord gave me such a peace about who he was calling me to be, so we began to study the word together. The dreams returned but I no longer put on my track shoes, instead I took them off and embraced what God was doing in me. (See Daniel 4:5)

Indicators: You're Meant to Serve Beside Him

Dreams and visions are one way I believe God shares his plans with you. He will at times give some of us a glimpse of what he is calling us to do. I never asked God to be called into ministry, my prayers were:

Lord, please show me my purpose.
Lord, why am I here in this earth suit?
What is it that you would have me to do while I'm here?

These were my constant prayers because I literally did not know why I was here. I always had this feeling, even as a young girl that I was going to do great things. We all are great and greatness dwells within us lying dormant until it is awakened by the will and determination to fulfill your God given purpose.

Scriptures that Encouraged Me

"May he grant your heart's desires and make all your plans succeed." Psalm 20:4 NLT

"For I know the plans I have for you, declares the LORD, plans to prosper you and not to harm you, plans to give you hope and a future." Jeremiah 29:11 NLT

"Now all glory to God, who is able, through his mighty power at work within us, to accomplish infinitely more than we might ask or think." Ephesians 3:20 NLT

"But forget all that it is nothing compared to what I am going to do. For I am about to do something new. See, I have already begun! Do you not see it? I will make a pathway through the wilderness. I will create rivers in the dry wasteland." Isaiah 43:18-19 NLT

Understanding your Assignment

First Ladies and women in general, we all have an assignment while we are here in the earth. Whether you fulfil that assignment or not is up to you. God has given each one of us gifts and talents, and a measure of faith which enables us to seek out our God given assignment or purpose. In order to accomplish what God has assigned, we must understand our assignment. Your God given assignment is the assignment you didn't ask for, however the Lord drafted you for the job because he knew you would be the right fit for the team. Understand this, you can feel like you're doing what God is calling you to do and carrying out your assignment because you are helping to meet the needs of the ministry, when in fact you are just keeping busy.

When I started my Christian journey, I was so excited I wanted to do everything in the church. Where ever they needed help, I was ready, willing and eager to volunteer. I was a single soldier. I had no children and was in a job that allowed me the flexibility to work in ministry. One day, we had a meeting and they were looking for help in the transportation ministry, so I volunteered to help in that area as well. After the meeting as I was preparing to leave the grounds, one of the members of the transportation ministry came up to me and said, "The pastor understands you want to help out, but he has to put a stop to you joining everything and being all over the place." I looked at him and said, "Okay," then I turned and walked away.

While driving home I began to weep and ask God what was so wrong about wanting to serve and help where there was a need. I cried and prayed all the way home. Later that evening the Lord gave me a peace about it. What the pastor didn't realize is I was doing my best to help me stay grounded because temptation was all around me and being in the military made it that much easier to slip back into old habits. Being delivered and staying delivered is two different things. Nevertheless, after talking with my mother about the situation, she said, "Find the area that you love and work in it and don't worry about the rest. It's okay, nobody can do everything. You still need a life because I need a son-in-law and some grandkids before I am too old to enjoy them."

After she finished prophesying (chuckle), I woke up the next morning with a brand-new outlook about the situation. I began to pray and ask God where He would have me to work in the ministry where I could serve Him best. It was through the process of many mornings and nights of prayer and allowing God to speak to me and show me where my passion really was. I was already working in the Youth Ministry, but God began to show me how he saw his children being ministered to and giving me the creative ideas and direction.

His vision clearly was larger than life to me. A vision I definitely did not feel or think I was capable of doing at all. I felt inadequate as a leader. I was still learning, and this was totally different from my experience as a soldier and leading troops. It became so clear that I had to work and study just as

I did in the military for promotions. I made sure I was attending Bible Study and Sunday School, all of the Women's Ministry events. This time, it wasn't to get promoted but to get better. One thing I learned from my parents and in the military was very strong work ethic, therefore I put my all into any an everything I did for the Lord. I was an outstanding soldier in the Army, so my thought process was if you can give Uncle Sam your best, surely you can do it for the Lord! I accepted my assignment quickly and was glad to be in a role that suited me, where my passion burned like a heated furnace for the young people.

I cannot express to you enough first ladies how important it is to grow your relationship with God, develop a lifestyle of prayer, fasting and worship. It is in those intimate times we have with God where he holds us close in his arms while we bask in his presence and listen to his still small voice. His voice is one of comfort, peace, instructions, chastisement, but most of all love. It is wise to seek God in every decision we make, and I can be the first one to admit there have been times when I moved prematurely and payed for it in the end. I've learned to slow down and not allow the excitement of an idea to cause me to move hastily.

People will push you into doing things and as soon as you start succeeding or surpassing them then that jealous demon begins to show up. You need your own one-on-one time with the Lord. It makes handling the challenges with decision making easier especially when you are carrying out your God given assignment.

I thank God I didn't get discouraged by man and was able to take constructive criticism and move on. What happened after that was all in God's plan. After being exposed to God's plan, I really didn't have time for the other ministries and God worked it out in my favor! Working in the Youth Ministry is where the Lord allowed my husband to find me. *Praise break!*

Accepting Your Assignment

Being a young pastor's wife started out a little rocky, of course. I really didn't know what to expect, and this is why mentorship is important. I believe every young pastor's wife needs guidance from a seasoned, experienced first lady. There is a gamut of things that can be and should be gleaned from them. They can't teach you how to become the first lady God called you to be, but they can instruct you on the tools needed to be the best first lady you can be. It is important to connect with someone that has been where you are trying to go. For instance, if you want to have an effective women's ministry connect with a first lady that has succeeded in that area. In doing so, it provides the opportunity to share insights and learning experiences with one another.

This type of collaboration helps to enhance mutual effectiveness and minimizes the possibility of failure and disappointment along the way. There is so much good that can derive from having that significant lady of wisdom and knowledge that has walked in the shoes you are barely stepping high in. The synergy in sharing scriptures, thought provoking ideas and the wisdom from walking daily beside the pastor in leadership should never be discounted or taken for granted. I have discovered in my eight years of serving in the vineyard of ministry as first lady that many of the things we go through in today's church they went through when I was growing up in church.

Receiving guidance from a seasoned first lady takes the guess work out of so many things. There is really no need for trial and error. People are looking for realness and a tangible leader they can touch, someone that is authentic, so they can embrace the gospel and how it has worked in another first lady's life.

First ladies face many challenges as you virtually are on display like a fish in a fishbowl. The added stress and pressure of being on display can also be fearful, therefore you need someone that can help you understand those feelings and teach you how to redirect those feelings and bring them under subjection. It can be overwhelming at times, but like my first lady told me prayer is the best answer I can give and trust God. Having that go to person to talk to when the winds of life and ministry are blowing, and at the same time you need the voice of reason to keep you from doing or saying some things you will regret.

CHAPTER SIX

Importance of a Support System

IT IS IMPORTANT TO HAVE a support team because there are times when you need to steal away and be yourself and let your hair down. You are expected to have it all together, be on point at all times, dress right and be flawless. Operating in the role of first lady can be stressful, fearful and very eventful, therefore having that strong support group helps bring balance when you are also a ministry leader. Having someone close to you and supporting you in ministry doing kingdom work frees you up to do other things within the ministry.

These people have a vested interest in supporting the ministry, the ministry vision and the first lady because they understand the weight she carries to fulfill her role. The truth of the matter is, if no one else can do it, if no one else can be at the meeting, or attend the service supporting the pastor it is up to the first lady to get it done. Your support system doesn't always have to come from within your ministry community however that is the community we gravitate to because our lives are basically built around it. My husband's job is there; our children's friends are there, and my social network is all in our church community. It's a part of it.

There are pros and cons to having a support group just within the church community. When a conflict arises, or something goes bad, it is often difficult to approach because the role is no longer friend or brother, it is pastor and leader. Some people cannot handle it when the pastor must correct or rebuke. When it happens, the pastor and his family, the family involved, and the church community suffers. With our lives encompassed within the church, it makes us vulnerable. For instance, if my husband loses his job, we lose our support group and community. My husband did not lose his job; however, we have experienced a disruption in our community and support team. Having had this experience allowed us to re-evaluate how we were building our community and support group. It is important to have an outside support team, so your entire community of support doesn't get de-railed or crumbles.

CHAPTER SEVEN

Self-Awareness & Self-Care

The Importance of being Self-Aware

BEING SELF-AWARE MEANS having conscious knowledge of one's own character and feelings. In other words, you know who you are and whose you are. Knowing who you are gives you the confidence you need to walk worthy of your calling. As my pastor says all the time, "Your video ought to match your audio!" "And I am certain that God, who began the good work within you, will continue his work until it is finally finished on the day when Christ Jesus returns," according to Philipians6:1 NLT. Be confident in who you are, and the assignment God has called you to. God knows all about you, he made the delicate, inner parts of your body and knit you together in your mother's womb. Even on your dark days, God still knows you. (See Psalm 139)

Once you realize that God called you to Queen status as a wife, mother, woman in ministry, first lady; your destiny is already preordained, and he waits patiently on us to embrace our calling. We can learn this from First Lady, Esther who wasn't born in that role. Through life circumstances and love for her people, it caused her to rise and embrace who God already said she would be. "With the help of God, she gained the confidence she needed to go before the King, risking her very life for the people of God whom she loved unconditionally." Esther 5:1-7,10 NLT

We are no different than Esther in many aspects. We weren't born first lady's, we married into the role, that lets me know God's hand was in it because the word of God says a man that finds a wife, finds a good thing and obtains favor from the Lord! When God gave me the revelation, I stopped kicking and screaming like a child begging God for a different assignment. I have seen to many other first ladies that just weren't happy about their assignment and those that really embraced their role. I felt unworthy because those ladies had endured some things I believed I couldn't endure, at the time. As an incoming first lady, I knew God was still working on me; you can say I needed just a little more Jesus because I didn't want to do it.

Personally, I would have laid unholy hands on some people for messing with my man. Although he is the pastor, he is my man first. I mean my *husband*. Some people reading this are so holy and will take what I just said out of context. Seriously speaking, it is extremely important to your walk and the success of the ministry God has called you and your husband to lead that you as the first lady have a level of understanding and confidence in knowing that God chose you. You were the best woman for the job to help support his son. Bring to the table of ministry your contribution of substance; an unexplainable love for the people, a deep commitment and reverence to please God by supporting the pastor one hundred percent. Remember, you are in the glass fishbowl and everyone is watching.

If you contribute negativity, the members will think that it is okay to do the same thing. So, speak positive, be encouraging and loving because you matter and what you do matters to your husband, and to God. Does this mean you won't get frustrated or angry? No, it doesn't but you must remember you are the *queen* and God holds the heart of the king in his hands. "The king's heart is like a stream of water directed by the LORD; he guides it wherever he pleases. People may be right in their own eyes, but the LORD examines their heart. The LORD is more pleased when we do what is right and just than when we offer him sacrifices." Proverbs 21:1-3 NLT

Importance of Self-Care

When you embrace your role and the assignment given by God in ministry there must be time for preparation, sanctification and rejuvenation. Taking care of yourself is extremely vital to not only your husband's success but your success as well. If you don't do a good job of taking care of your fearfully and wonderfully made temple, how do you think that will affect your husband? It will affect him a great deal because he can't do what he is called to do if you're ill. I didn't grasp this concept in the beginning, all I knew was I was a woman in a leadership role and if it meant sacrificing getting my hair or nails done, then I would make the sacrifice. I would go without getting the proper rest, praying and seeking God for fresh creative ideas for my area of responsibility, so the pastor would not have to be concerned about my area of responsibility. I wanted it to run like a well-oiled machine because I was the first lady and that was what I was supposed to do.

Then one day, the light bulb went off and I began to look around and take notice of some things. Everyone else's hair was fried, dyed, laid to the side, and mine was pulled back in a ponytail or looking like a bush needing a relaxer; nails and feet on point, clothes up to date. People are vacationing not staycationing, visiting family, friends, college buddies, going on cruises, the whole nine. Every month someone is alerting us that they won't be in service this Sunday or the next weekend or the next week, and I'm thinking *I've been here since inception and haven't been on a real family vacation that didn't include a church conference.*

Those things may sound trivial to some, but from a first lady's perspective, it is not. We neglect living for ourselves many times because we spend a lot of our time living for someone else. It is the agape love and compassion for the people that compels us to reach out and show love to all. We want to do our best to try and mimic the heartbeat of the pastor.

You can run yourself in the ground trying to please and appease people only to find yourself on a sick bed and those same people have moved on from your ministry. People may not return the same compassion you have shown them. It doesn't matter because you are a leader and leaders must be prepared to make the necessary sacrifices in ministry. God wants us to do well and be in good health even as our soul prospers.

Preparation

Preparation is the action or process of making ready or being made ready for use or consideration. It is not an option. You never go into a setting where the spotlight is on you and you're not prepared to deliver your speech, right? If you were a runway model, you'd rehearse and rehearse until your strut is just right. Preparing and transitioning are synonymous. You must take time for personal development by reading other material besides the bible and the commentary; it helps you stay relevant and exercises your brain.

According to Readers Digest, Yale researchers reported "Chapter books encourage *deep reading*. Unlike, say, skimming a page of headlines, reading a book (of any genre) forces your brain to think critically and make connections from one chapter to another, and to the outside orld." (Specktor, 2016). Word power is brain power which is needed for the multifaceted role as first lady and minister. You must be prepared for the door of opportunity to open. God will open doors for you when he knows you are ready to walk through them. Feeding the spiritual man is just as important as feeding the natural.

Sanctification

Sanctification is defined as, "The state of proper functioning." To sanctify someone or something is to set that person or thing apart for the use intended by its designer. A pen is *sanctified* when used to write. Eyeglasses are *sanctified* when used to improve sight. In the theological sense, things are sanctified when they are used for the purpose God intends. A human being is sanctified, therefore, when he or she lives according to God's design and purpose." (www.biblestudytools.com).

I couldn't have said it any better. It is a clarion call for all the saints who have been called by God to start walking in their purpose. Often women will say to me, "I couldn't be married to a preacher, nose turned up and rolling their eyes."

Or they will say, "I don't know how you do it." "I couldn't be no first lady," speaking very sarcastically to me.

This reminds me of a sermon I once preached titled, "It's in my DNA!" Our divine design is for the master to use us for his glory. Greatness dwells in of all of us, but it is especially important that first ladies answer the call and are **D**esigned **N**aturally **A**wesome! God is our designer and living a life exemplifying holiness and character according to the word of God is our purpose. We must understand that we have been set apart, so God's plan can be carried out in our lives throughout his Kingdom. Just because we see someone else doing something that doesn't mean we should do it, too. Ladies, let's commit to following God's design for our lives.

Rejuvenation

Rejuvenation is to make young again; restore to youthful vigor, appearance, et.

Being well-groomed is another area of being prepared. Take the time to keep your hair styled and looking fresh. Visit the hair salon and allow yourself to relax while someone with anointed hands wash and massage your scalp. There is nothing wrong with being pampered every woman should like to get a massage every now and again. This is a great way to decompress and relieve stress. Working in ministry can wear you done and out especially if you are in the building stage or your ministry is small, when wearing more than one hat is common. Taking time for yourself is important to be a successful first lady while serving in ministry alongside of your husband. Your body must be able to keep up with the demand of the ministry. You can't properly serve others in the Kingdom if you are tired all the time, and over extended due to busyness. This is due to a lack of balance; when we lack balance, it opens the door for being overworked and under achievers.

Our dreams and vision become stagnant because our physical bodies are suffering. An unhealthy diet and not getting proper rest can lead to illness. Our bodies have everything we need within it, designed by God to be self-renewing, self-cleansing and self-healing however it must be feed the proper diet. Retreating for rejuvenation is fuel for the mind, body and soul. Our God is a redeemer, let the redeemed of the Lord say so!

8 Self-Care Tips

In the past few years, I made a conscious decision to make a lifestyle change because I desire to live an abundant, happy, healthy and wealthy life. I chose the term abundant because it encompasses so much, not just money and stuff. Many of us have a lot of stuff in abundance but it does not make you happy. Living a healthy life is important to me and one of my number one goals. Last year I was able to shed thirty pounds, so I wouldn't have to use diabetic medication for the rest of my life. Now, I'm believing God to shed another thirty, to reach my goal of a healthier me: physically, spiritually, naturally, and financially.

Tip 1: Identify the areas of weaknesses in your life that you want to improve. You want to strengthen your weaknesses and maintain your strengths. You must be prepared to combat the enemy at any given time. Maintaining your spiritual strength is the most valuable aspect you can have when you are anointed by God to a work in his Kingdom.

Tip 2: Make a commitment to spend at least thirty minutes breathing, and if you need support, ask your accountability partner to hold you to your commitment. First ladies are unique individuals. We are expected to look a certain way, act a certain way and do certain things. I debunk that myth. God holds us accountable for what he has given, so it is okay to breathe and not feel pressured by people's expectations. Breathing exercises help you see things more clearly. When the weight of your assignment becomes overwhelming, you need to breathe. (See 1 King 19)

I steal away to the bathroom, my car, the altar to close my eyes and breathe in and out very slowly for about five minutes. Then I pour my heart out to God. (See Psalm 61:2-3)

Tip 3: Schedule an appointment to see a nutritionist or do some research on eating a well-balanced diet. Keeping your temple should be a priority for you. If your temple is not physically fit it makes it more difficult to carry the weight of your assignment as a first lady. The anointing cost and you will face spiritual and physical battles on this journey. Temple preparation is a must! (See 1 Corinthians 3:16)

Tip 4: Take long walks. Taking long walks not only helps with your blood flow (cardiovascular system), it also helps with soul searching, reassessment, recalibrating, problem solving and gathering yourself because as your blood flows your mind flows. (See Psalm 23).

Tip 5: Invest in self-improvement by attending trainings and seminars specifically for first ladies. This will help you walk in your calling, provide guidance, leadership skills, networking opportunities that enable you to glean from other first ladies and enhance your knowledge of your assignment. Self-improvement also helps you feel accomplished as you achieve higher learning. This is important for how you perceive yourself; your self-worth. (See 2 Timothy 2:5)

Tip 6: Seek Professional counseling, Ladies! It is okay to have someone outside of your circle to express your thoughts and feelings with. A person that can and will help you bring things into perspective by assisting you with working through your issues in a safe space, someone who is safe to be vulnerable with. Counselors are licensed professionals and bound by law to maintain client confidentiality unless you plan on harming yourself or one of your church members. Otherwise, full disclosure is in order.

Let me testify to you concerning the power of seeking professional help. My counselor Mrs. S. Murphy. God orchestrated every session and she was able to relate to me being a pastor's wife and serving in ministry. It is nothing to be ashamed of because God wants all of us, not bits and pieces, because we are frayed from our past. Be the first to admit you need help and get the help you need; your mind, body and soul will thank you for it. Your family will love you even the more for it. (See Psalm 16:70 and Proverbs 12:15)

Tip 7: Retail therapy and lunch with your girls. When all else fails, go shopping!!! Be wise, window shopping is great retail therapy, too. If you make any purchases be sure the money is allotted in your budget. Spend time browsing and laughing, this helps you get away from it all for a few hours. Establish ground rules, no talking about church! This is all about letting your hair down, relaxing and laughing, not necessarily spending money. (See James 1:5)

Tip 8: If you don't have a journal, get you one. Journaling works wonders for your mind and your soul. Writing your thoughts, dreams and vision, even in times when you are frustrated and angry. Write it down and release it on paper. You will find by writing things down, asking God to help you through them or teaching you how to overcome certain things; when he answers your prayers, you can go back and see how far you have come. You can clearly see how much God has blessed you and kept you from sinning, going down the wrong path, saying the wrong things and kept you in right fellowship with your brothers and sisters in Christ.

CHAPTER EIGHT

Church Culture

LET'S TAKE A BROADER LOOK. Church culture is the atmosphere in which the church functions or how the organization does things. The culture of the church helps shape who we are and who we become. Growing up in a promising ministry located in a rural area, the culture at the time was centered around leadership beliefs and values. The culture was founded on doctrinal statements and denominational values promoting all it components.

My church was a very traditional Baptist Church with a very strong belief system and went to great lengths to ensure the youth of the future were getting the Christian Education they needed. They rewarded us for our efforts and participation. We didn't have Children's Church, Youth Service or Youth Sunday where the children lead the worship service. We had Bible Study, Youth Choir, Sunday School,

Youth Ushers, Circle K and Baptist Training Union which we participated in faithfully.

Education was drilled in us and stamped into our minds, so we would not forget the importance of *knowledge being power*. This is the one thing that helped shape me into the woman I am today along with the church mothers. Those church mothers didn't play with us at all. There was no horse playing in the house of God, you sat down, you didn't chew gum and you didn't get up to go to the bathroom while the word was going forth. You didn't wear anything in the church because if you did, they would pull you to the side and tell you, "Baby, you need some more material with that skirt." My mother sang in the choir and she would make us sit on the second row and would give my brother and I the speech, "If I have to come out of that choir stand, I know something!" We were like statutes on the second row, we didn't flinch.

These same principles shape the church culture along with doing things in a timely manner, being organized and functioning as a healthy body. If it wasn't for the discipline I learned at an early age, I would not have the discipline I have now when it comes to the Lord and ministry. I'm not perfect by far, but I am striving to be the best I can be.

When you understand the culture of your ministry, it will help you grow, love and serve wholeheartedly. Case and point, if your church culture is built on precision and strong organizational skills, you know that you can't halfway plan an event and expect the pastor or leadership to bless it without full disclosure. Understanding the culture also helps to identify strengths and weakness within the ministry. Remember, I said the church culture is the way you do things (Chand, Samuel 2011). The way an organization functions can help or hinder the growth of the ministry. You can't be a church that is just putting things down on paper and never carrying those things out. If you're going to talk the talk, walk the walk. It has helped me better understand the importance of church culture as it relates to our ministry. We're a church that loves God and his people. We teach the word of God by the aid of the Holy Spirit, so the broken are mended and the lost are found, that we all inherit the Kingdom of God. Our culture says we win!

I know that I can serve in the capacity of empowering the women to pursue their destiny, so they too can win. I know that by serving in a leadership role I have an opportunity to love on the people of God by being touchable and relevant. Knowing the culture helps with all the moving parts and learning where to serve best and where I can be productive is key to any organization. I feel that as women in leadership it is important that we help identify our ministry culture. Why? We are verbal creatures and we can see things because we pay attention to everything. Women are also very emotional creatures and if we're not careful, can be busybodies keeping a bunch of mess going in the church.

You should be able to identify if your church culture is healthy or unhealthy; it makes a huge difference in people deciding to stay or go. It may be one or two people that do not understand the culture of the church and do not demonstrate the love that's been established among the people and might be the only person or persons a visitor encounters. A visitor can immediately identify the church as one that doesn't show love to the people.

If you are a small ministry without an edifice, and you are in a storefront or having service in a tent on the land the church purchased, then people may think your church culture is unstable. If ex-members are running the church in the ground because they left the ministry and they are telling a one-sided story, their version of why they left then people may think your church culture is sowing discord and messy.

It's not right, but it happens. No matter how many times the pastor asks you to greet your neighbor in love, some just will not do it. According to Church Executive (2011), "The strongest force in an organization is not vision or strategy, it is the culture which holds all the other components." You want to know why the ministry isn't farther along than you think it should be, look at your church culture. How you do things in your ministry matters and how you treat those that work and are united with your ministry speaks, especially how women are treated in the church.

First ladies, church culture can assist with our development in the ministry and our service to God.

Women are also creatures of habit and often predictable but as the culture of the church is being defined you will find yourself doing your best to ensure the culture is healthy. You won't allow the enemy show up and show out on your watch. You find your spiritual senses becoming more keen and sensitive to the Holy Spirit, and anything that may try to disrupt the culture that has been established in the ministry, you will have the holy boldness to bring that spirit under subjection.

Church Culture

Establishing and maintaining a healthy culture within the ministry means your prayer life will increase, organizational skills will increase, communication skills will increase, and hospitality skills will increase. We must evolve in ministry and continue to strive for greater. You can't be in your feelings all the time and want to fall out and throw in the towel. Ministry takes courage, tenacity, strength both physical and spiritual to combat the enemy. If you fall out with anybody let it be the adversary. Ladies, we matter in ministry and our spiritual growth will reveal if we are serious about ministry or just doing enough to get by. Church culture sniffers will sniff that out and will determine that your church culture isn't serious about training their ministry leaders. Everything matters that we do in our ministries. You can get angry, upset and even mad, but it is a fact, your role as a woman in ministry can help or hurt the ministry.

CHAPTER NINE

The Role & Importance of Women in Ministry

I CAN GET MAD ALL OVER AGAIN at the thought of my role as a wife, in the home, on the job, in ministry, in the community and in the world, but I won't. It may get frustrating at times, but I wouldn't change a thing. Life can be very demanding especially when we do our best trying to wear all the hats we wear and the different roles we play, and the lives affected by how well we play them. It can be tough to maintain balance as a wife, you have your wifely obligations and duties to your husband, children and the home. Honey, I would be lying if I said everything has been all good since day one.

I was a mess! I had been single so long I didn't know how to enjoy the fruits of being married nor did I know how to let him love me the way a husband should love his wife.

My background had a great deal to do with how I reacted to certain things. I was raised in a home where both parents worked outside the home. I was the oldest child and had the responsibility of making sure my little brother was cared for after school until my mom came home.

My father was a man's man. He was hardworking, avid outdoorsman who enjoyed going hunting and fishing to keep us fed, and he believed we needed to know the value of hard work. He would always say, "If a man doesn't work, he doesn't eat." We had chores daily and weekend duties.

My mother taught us that family is everything, family is all you have in this world other than the Lord, and family sticks together. She taught us how to love and be content with what God has blessed us with. Both of my parents have big hearts and although my father was very stern, he would still give you the shirt off his back if he could. They believed in both my brother and I becoming productive citizens and not depending on people to give us a hand out. Mom would say to both of us, "You can do anything you set your mind to and you can be whoever you want to be." All those life lessons stuck with me and when it was my turn to take on the world I went for it. We didn't have a lot of money growing up so there were a lot of things I missed out on or, so I thought. I joined the army to finish completing college and to have the extra money to help my parents with my brother. My parents were loving and kind-hearted people and have been married almost thirty years. I can honestly say, that if they really argued they didn't do it in front of us.

After the army, I was very militant. I was used to doing things on my own and by myself. I forgot that we married each other to help each other. I had to learn to accept his help and respect him in his role as my husband as I embraced my role as his helpmeet.

Losing respect for one's husband can be detrimental to a marriage and seems to happen in long marriages more than one might imagine. It's as if the love you have lasts but the respect precedes the love. This is a hurtful thing for a man to endure, so as his wife you are required by God to respect your husband. Ephesians 5:33 NLT reads, "So again I say, each man must love his wife, and wife must respect her husband." Husbands have their role and wives we have our role to play. Many times, we find ourselves lost in the part we are supposed to be playing due to life situations and circumstances. Sometimes we can be blind, and the lines become blurred as to how a marriage is supposed to work. Know your role and live it out to the fullest. Don't be the one that has lost their manuscript and their way to be a successful woman, in marriage, on your job, at home with co-workers at church and in the world.

Are you that woman that is cast in this movie called life and you are basically going through the motions because you have mastered your lines as a wife, mother, co-worker, in your community and in the world. That has got to be a lonely, empty place because there is nothing to fulfill your role if you are not the leading lady, the star, the Queen. You were blessed with the part during casting call, you showed up and were blessed by God, now it is your time to shine. It can be difficult to shine if you are not happy about your role. Life is too short to go through it and never fulfill your role as woman on this earth.

I'm mad because I see too many ladies taking a back seat to Benny BoBo and allow him to shine as if he was the star in your movie. He won't pay a bill, take you on a date and pay the bill, cook you a meal, wash your car that he is driving and dropping you off at work, he eating up your groceries, sucking up your AC and heat, can't buy a ring, won't put a ring on it, but yet he is in center stage in your life and your life is passing you by. You are the star in this movie! Women it's time to kick the extras out the door and take your rightful place center stage, you are important and your role matters.

If I had fell in that trap set by the enemy, I would not be where I am today. I can honestly say I am excited about my life and where God has me although it has been a long road to travel and I've had some hard pills to swallow. God has been good! Without my upbringing, trials and tribulations, I would not be able to show up in the world as a woman, an Ambassador for Christ, who walks worthy of the call of first lady. All first ladies pause and toot your horn! If you are a wife and a mother working in ministry faithfully, toot your horn. Now, everybody toot your horn at the same time and say it loud, "*I am a Woman of Importance!*"

Importance of Women

I know some of you are wondering why I chose the title *Diary of a Mad First Lady*. Understand, I'm not the only first lady that is mad, I'm the one that chose to put my thoughts and heart on paper. The world view of women should make you uneasy enough to do something. Women are undervalued, under paid, misunderstood, portrayed as sex symbols on TV, even on the commercials that advertise food. The world will try to make you think the only successful women are movie stars, music artist, philanthropist, models or part of a royal family. This has gone on for decades. Slowly but surely, women are evolving and have made tremendous strides to make their mark on the world and its systems.

Who we are as women speaks volumes. We are nurturers, it is in our nature to care for others. We don't mind making the sacrifice to make sure our family is fed and comfortable. We will go the extra to put a smile on our children's faces. In ministry we will make the necessary sacrifice and adjustment for things to run smoothly, just so nothing is added to our husband's plate. We have a servant's heart. We jump in to lend a hand to scrub toilets, usher, sing in the women's choir, lead devotion, drive the church van, preach if we're called to that portion of ministry, teach and anything else needed for ministry to go forth. We want God to be glorified.

"Woman is sacred, a woman who loves is holy," Alexandre Dumas. The very essence of a woman is her passion, gentle nature and her ability to love unconditionally. Women can bring calmness to calamity, help to the helpless and clarity to those areas that maybe misunderstood while, at times, suffering in silence. However, despite what we are going through, we know how to express gratitude and apologize often times when we are not the one in the wrong. That doesn't mean we never mess up. There are times when you allow your gentle side to go out the window and the old you will show up if the right button gets pushed. When that happens then we don't want to apologize. I'm trying to help somebody right here, right now. It is not worth it. They are not worth it. Remain who you are and move forward. Remember, you are sacred and holy, and an earthen vessel filled with treasures. *"But we have this treasure in earthen vessels, that the excellency of the power may be of God, and not of us."* 2 Corinthians 4:7 NLT

Women are valuable and when we show up, we don't show up empty handed. We show up with our hands full and ready to put them to work using wisdom, knowledge and substance to every situation in ministry and the marketplace. Let me enlighten you as to how important you *truly* are.

You are so important to God that he had to perform the first surgery on man removing a rib bone as he took his time to divinely design women, fearfully and wonderfully made. He shaped and molded a lump of clay and just one rib creating beauty that he could be proud of. The master keeps us on the wheel completing every intricate detail, depositing everything in us to make us fit for the master's use. He loves you just that much and he didn't stop there. Even when Mother Eve did a nose dive and partook of the forbidden fruit, the Lord chastised and rebuked, but still showed love and compassion for who he created by blessing the lineage. So, ladies we are destined for success, it is in our DNA. Thanks to Father Abraham and the promises God made to him, our lineage history tells me we are joint heirs and from a family of royalty.

Yes, you may have been knocked down, counted out and told you were never good for anything, but laying on your back. I declare the works of the Lord over your life and denounce every demonic spirit that may try to come against you or the work of the Lord, it is bound and invalidated by the blood of Jesus Christ. You are IMPORTANT!

CHAPTER TEN

Victory Over It

Misunderstood and Not Having a Voice

DESPITE THE IMAGE portrayed by society, women are power-ful! One thing that really gets under my skin is when people try to discredit what women have to say or who they are in God. It has been my personal experience that some men can't handle the fact that God called women to preach the gospel. I will never forget the first time we went to my home church where I grew up. I will add, my mom still attends church there and shared with her then new pastor that my husband and I were called to start a ministry where we were both pastoring. He acknowledged my husband and invited him to the pulpit. My husband looked at me and I gave him a nod of approval because we had experienced this in other churches.

My husband joined him as I sat there about to burn in my seat with fury. If someone would have dropped an egg on my head, it would have fried hard. I began to pray and ask God what is it with these pastors that have an issue acknowledging your daughters? I was part of a ministry that acknowledged female ministers and they were allowed to exercise their gift.

As I sat there, the Lord calmed me, and I felt fury leave my eyes. I began to look around and over fifty percent of the church membership were women. It gets better. When we finally meet after church, he reaches his hand out and says to me, "God bless you *Sister* Boyd." I was thinking, *Wow, really? You are just gonna disregard who God says I am because of your traditional hang up with women preaching the Gospel?* That was what I was thinking, but I never disrespected the man of God.

On another occasion, I was invited to speak at a women's program for Mother's Day. When I arrived, that same pastor made it very plain that I was only speaking and not preaching. He said, "I know that's what y'all do in Georgia, but we don't do that here. You will be speaking to the women, but not from the pulpit, it will be in the Fellowship

Hall." I said, "Yes Sir," but God knows I wanted to shoot him with a prayer of deliverance! I walked away and headed to the Fellowship Hall feeling like what I had to say didn't matter and he was just appeasing the young lady that asked ~~for~~ me to come. The enemy almost had me thinking I was inadequate for the job and maybe this wasn't what God had for me to do, especially if this is what I had to look forward to. It was frustrating to know there were people that still carry on like that. To this day, he still calls me *Sister* Boyd.

I'm so over that now! I don't need his pulpit or any other pulpit to be heard by God or his people. Being a minster is not predicated on man allowing you to grace their pulpit, you can minister the gospel wherever God opens a door. When people try to stifle you or discount the content and character you bring by using your voice it can make you feel like you are not valued. Let me tell you right now, you are valuable to God and your voice matters. Why? God created us, and he gave us a mouth to use for his glory. Did you know women in ministry, wives, first ladies are so valuable to God he holds us in such high regard that he will not even listen to a man's prayers when he does not honor her as an equal heir in God's Kingdom. (See 1 Peter 3:7)

The importance of being understood, accepted and valued is major. Women being understood and accepted only enhances what they bring to the table in ministry, at home, on their jobs and in everyday life. We make the property value go up when we step on the grounds because we are women of worth! Many times, I think it is a misconception about women finding their place in the church. In the days of old, women were to keep silent in the church and in biblical times they sat in the back of the church. Society has evolved, and the culture of the church has changed tremendously. Seeking acceptance is just women saying *acknowledge who I am in God.*

Men have dominated every sport, corporate America, the pay scale in the military and in our churches. With this in mind, some women have often been left out or used to help the man get to where he is only to be forgotten. That is not all cases, but it is a very familiar story in many cases. God has valued women for years and sometimes I think that is forgotten.

When we look back through scripture, we find God used ordinary women to do extraordinary things.

It was Zipporah, Moses' wife that saved his life when God was going to punish him for refusing to follow his command concerning Israel, when he was to tell Pharaoh, "Let my son go, so he can worship me." (See Exodus 4:24-26)

Ruth is another good example. She refused to return home but chose to stay with her mother-in-law Naomi out of dedication and love for her. This bond led to the lineage of our Lord and Savior.

Mary is a great example of our value in the Kingdom of God because God used a single woman to carry his son in her womb, giving birth to his son Jesus so the world could see. He grew up, performed miracles, signs and wonders and laid down his life to save us all. Don't tell me we aren't valuable!

We are valuable because we are intelligent, we prioritize our lives, we are relentless, we are giving, resourceful, spiritually minded, but most of all, we fear God and reverence him. When we fear the Lord, we receive praises that are due to us, our handy work speaks for itself and produces good fruit that validates us and brings recognition. According to Proverbs 30-31 NLT, "Charm is deceptive, and beauty does not last; but a woman who fears the Lord will be greatly praised. Reward her for all she has done. Let her deeds publicly declare her praise."

There are benefits to serving God and being fully committed to him, no matter who accepts you or don't understand your value. If you ask me, people who think like that are misunderstood. Keep moving forward and pursuing the destiny God has for your life.

Wisdom from First Ladies

I TOOK THE LIBERTY of asking five first ladies if they have felt misunderstood or made to feel like they didn't have a voice in the ministry? For the sake of confidentiality, we're not disclosing their names here.

Faithful said: *I do feel misunderstood sometimes. I would say first by husband, the pastor, because when I am trying to protect him it has been misconstrued as jealousy. When all I want is for his good not to be evil spoken of. I also feel misunderstood by saints because I hurt, too. No one encourages me but expects to be lifted up; not vice versa.*

Honesty shared: *I feel like I do have a voice and the people in our ministry respect me as first lady.*

Love said: *Yes, sometimes I feel misunderstood, but I never feel like I don't have a voice. I wholeheartedly believe the role of women is necessary in the church.*

Grace said: *Yes, I have been misunderstood at times and perceived as mean and unapproachable. People may not know how to receive me because I am for the most part a serious person and my facial expressions may say one thing, but I mean something totally different than what they are thinking.*

Wisdom said: *Yes, sometimes. It could be my delivery or the audience, nonetheless, if God wants the message conveyed, I will have opportunity again.*

Next, I asked five women that work in ministry in various churches *why they believe women were important in the church?* It was very interesting to see what they had to say.

Why are Women Important to the Church?

Pure at heart said: *Women are important because they help carry, nurture, pray and support the vision. They also help provide much needed guidance and assistance to the male and female children, reinforcing the qualities their parents are instilling in them by providing Godly leadership and wisdom.*

Destiny said: I feel that women are important and often the backbone of many churches, but I do think that sometimes their significance is understated by many pastors because of the drastic need for men to step up.

Truth said: *Yes, the role of the women is very important in the church. Without women, the church would probably be empty. It takes strong, praying women that are fasting for the ministry and praying for their husbands, drawing them to Christ.*

Heaven sent said: *Women have played a vital part in every aspect of ministry. Even though some may believe that women shouldn't have a place in the church, God's word states that we are all one in Him. Galatians 3:28 says, "There is neither Jew not Greek, there is neither slave nor free man, there is neither male not female; for you are all one in Christ Jesus." Women's contribution is significant: women followed Jesus to care for his needs, women were the first to see the Lord risen and talk to him, and, women were prophetesses, evangelists, teachers and apostles. The church would never have survived throughout the ages without the support and encouragement of dedicated, Christian women!*

Serenity said: *Yes, I believe women have a purpose in the church, it is to be a help to the leaders and the pastor. When I think about when God created Eve for Adam, she was created to be his helpmate. The word of God says, "When a man finds a wife he finds a good thing and obtains Favor from the Lord." Proverbs 18:22 KJV. God did not want man to be alone, so God created us for man and to be helpers in his Kingdom.*

And, women have a way of reaching the heart of God through our obedience which can sometimes be a hard thing for man to do. We as women were created with a heart of compassion. Yes, women are needed. We can touch the heart of God with our prayers, praise and worship!

Meekness said: *Yes, I feel that women in the church are very important and significant, especially in this world today. Not that men are less, but we are considered as care givers and naturally compassionate. Men tend to show there compassion a little bit more through working and providing materialistically, but women show and give more of themselves in time, communication and listening. I feel this is a very good way of demonstrating AGAPE love to all. We can spread the love of Jesus in so many ways in the church, it is* much needed. I feel as women pull together and get on one accord, we can bring so many souls into the house of the Lord to be saved.

Just as Jesus sent Mary and many others out to spread the gospel not gossip, he too sends us as women in this world today to do the same.

Goodness said: Yes, God assigned a special role for women in the church. Women inspire, support, empower and encourage others. The church is deeply enriched through the presence and service of women.

Temperance said: I believe the role of women in the church is very important. We are leaders and examples for the younger women. Also, we can build up another sister and pour into their lives as well as share our experiences.

Dear Diary,

IF I HAD THE OPPORTUNITY to share with all first ladies across the nation, I would share with them these last few words. Love your husbands, they may not know everything but they do know you and who you are to them and who you are in God. Accept the role of first lady; embrace it, walk in it and enjoy the life God has given you. There is nowhere to go from here but up. You are not just another big hat sitting on the corner shelf of the church, to be pulled of the shelf when others feel it is time for us to speak. Your voice will be heard and understood. You are valuable to the Kingdom of God because God created woman to be a helpmeet. You are healthy and wealthy, and God has given you the ability to be a change agent by impacting the culture of your ministry and the lives of others around you. Your role as a woman is important and will not go unnoticed, not for selfish gain but so God can get all the Glory out of your life. Your role is important to you for your own growth and self-esteem, you are a woman of worth in God's eyesight. If it were not true he would not have chosen you for such an important assignment.

No more excuses. Understand your assignment, go forth with holy boldness and rise up first lady, rise up! God created you fearfully and wonderfully, and he placed the man of God in your life to fulfill your every prayer by blessing you with who and what you needed to complement each other. Continue to build that Godly relationship and be the example of a Godly marriage for your children and others. Leaving a legacy is important, therefore again I say, rise up first ladies, no more sticking your head in the sand. Believe in yourself, exercise your God confidence and rise up!

I refuse to be a *Mad First Lady* because it doesn't stop people from doing what they are going to do when their mind is made up. It doesn't stop people from hurting you or talking about you or your husband. Remind yourself God is in control and nothing happens except he allows it to happen in your life. They talked about Jesus and worse therefore if we have made the declaration we want to be like Christ, his words are true, and we too will suffer persecution. Although it may be hard and the road may get rough, just know you can make it because you are not only a Godly woman, you are a first lady walking in your God given assignment fulfilling your purpose and destiny as you serve in ministry beside your husband. God has Designed You Naturally Awesome!

My Prayer for You

Father, I thank you for blessing the hands that are holding this book. Keep them in your ever-loving care as you continue to watch over them on their journey in life, working diligently to fulfill the call to be a first lady, whether in ministry or in their homes. Lord, I pray that you will speak to this awesome woman of God with clarity as she seeks your face for guidance and direction on how to serve in her role while undergirding her husband in prayer as he leads your sheep. I ask that you continue to bless her with your wisdom and knowledge, releasing her full potential and creativity as she leads your daughters to a more successful, stronger and faithful walk with you meeting every need, so she will have neither need or want but good success in all that she puts her heart and mind to do. In Jesus name, Amen!

Did You Know?

- 25% of pastors' wives see their husband's work schedule as a source of conflict.

- 40% of pastors and 47% of spouses are suffering from burnout, frantic schedules, and/or unrealistic expectations.

- 45% of pastors' wives say the greatest danger to them and their family is physical, emotional, mental, and spiritual burnout.

- 56% of pastors' wives say that they have no close friends.

- 88% of pastor's wives have admitted to having periods of depression since being in ministry.

- 65% of the respondents feel fairly well equipped to be effective as pastors' wives.

- 43% stated the first most rewarding fact is "Seeing people grow in Christ."

- 26% stated the second most rewarding aspect of being a pastor's wife was "Teamwork with my husband."

- Ninety-four percent said their children "never" or "seldom" complain about being "PK's" (preachers' kids).

- 21 percent said they would not change anything; they are happy as they are.

- 59 percent say church commitments limit family time

- 19 percent would like to be thought of as an individual rather than always referred to as "the pastor's wife"; would like to be considered human rather than having to be perfect; and would like to be free of the stereotyped expectations of the congregation.

- 13 percent longed for freedom to express their true talents in jobs of their own choosing at church.

- The single biggest problem facing pastors' wives is that of friendship. Fifty-six percent said they do not have close friends in the church. For some (28 percent), this is intentional.

- 72 percent say their spouse has experienced resistance in the church.

- 69 percent say they have few people they can confide in.

- 68 percent worry about having enough money for retirement.

- 59 percent say church commitments limit family time.

- 49 percent say, "If I were honest at church about my prayer needs, they would just become gossip."

- 93 percent believe their spouse is a good fit for the present church.

- 90 percent think ministry has had a positive effect on their family.

- 85 percent say, "The church we serve takes good care of us."

- 83 percent enjoy their ministry work.

- 79 percent are satisfied with their role in ministry.

Declarations

As I speak over your life, I speak over my life.

You are who God says you are if you only believe.

You are valuable and filled with treasure.

You are a woman of influence and integrity.

You are powerful, yet full of grace.

You are anointed and appointed by God to do his will.

You will no longer walk in fear or doubt.

You are healed, delivered and free.

You are free from past hurts, wounds, guilt and shame.

You will no longer walk in need, lack or want,

You will use your God given ability to obtain wealth and own your own happiness.

You are one of God's master pieces ready to be put in the game.

Release the past and embrace the future, Rise up first lady_____ (put your name in the blank)

God is calling your name!

References

Pastor's Burnout. (2012) https://www.burnout.com

PaFstor's Spouses experience mixed blessings. (2017)
https://www.lifewayresearch.com

From the heart of a pastor's wife. https://www.fromthe-
heartofapastorswife

A Survey of minister's wives. https://www.christianityto-
day.com

About the Author

Elisha Boyd is the proud wife of Senior Pastor Daniel Boyd and together they serve as shepherds of Emmanuel Christian Church, located in Richmond Hill, GA. They have two children Danika and Nathaniel Boyd. She received a Bachelor of Science Degree from Columbia College in Business Management with a concentration in Human Resources and recently earned a Master of Arts in Human Services Counseling with a concentration in Military Resiliency from Liberty University. She is a certified Professional Life Coach, empowering women to take back their lives after being exposed to sexual trauma and living with Post Traumatic Stress Disorder. She is a dynamic Conference speaker and Vision Board trainer. She is currently employed by the Department of Veterans where she continues to make a difference in the lives of veterans, the surrounding community and countless others.

Co-Pastor Boyd also serves as Women of Worship Leader for the Women's Ministry where God has gifted her to preach, teach, train and encourage women to pursue their destiny. She plays an intricate role in the intercessory prayer ministry. God has given her a deep passion and desire for aiding teen girls through "NIARA", Young Women of High Purpose, a mentoring program the Lord gave her a vision for. She is involved in community support groups such as the Family Promise, NAACP of Bryan County, Support parent for the Richmond Hill High School Lady Wildcats and Lady Legacy AAU basketball teams. Her entrepreneurial spirit has led her to establish several startup businesses; Lisa's Chimichanga's and Joint Heirs Enterprise and T-shirt designing. She is also a Director III for Melaleuca, the Wellness Company. She founded Kingdom Women, a Non-profit Organization birthed to unite pastor wives and women for the common goal of advancing God's Kingdom.

Made in the USA
Columbia, SC
15 September 2021

44926259R00071